THE DIGITAL DIRT WORLD

LUKE EGGEBRAATEN

DEDICATION

I have to give all thanks to God and the amazing people He has put in my life. Nothing is possible without Him and I am forever grateful. I have been so incredibly blessed with all of the support surrounding me from my wife, Olivia, my family, friends, clients, community, and everyone who has been there since the beginning. From the bottom of my heart, thank you all.

The Digital Dirt World
Copyright © 2023 Luke Eggebraaten
Self-published
luke@phasermarketing.com
All rights reserved.
No part of this publication may be reproduced, stored in a retrieval system, stored in a database and / or published in any form or by any means, electronic, mechanical, photocopying, recording or otherwise, without the prior written permission of the publisher.

TABLE OF CONTENTS

INTRODUCTION	1
ONE	5
TWO	13
THREE	17
FOUR	27
FIVE	32
SIX	46
SEVEN	66
EIGHT	70
NINE	74
TEN	84
ELEVEN	92
TWELVE	103
THIRTEEN	112

INTRODUCTION

AN INTRODUCTION OF WHO I AM, WHO THIS BOOK IS FOR, AND WHAT WE'RE GOING TO COVER

What's up ya dirt bags?

I have been looking forward to this moment for a long time. You, holding this book, "The Digital Dirt World" is a dream come true for me and I hope it will mean something to you by the end, too. When determining the direction for this book, I had to stop and ask myself many times who I was actually writing this book for. Who is going to be my main audience? Is this the book that my family and friends are going to re-read every New Year? Probably not. Is this the book that will reinvent the wheel of digital marketing as we know it? Not necessarily.

This book is written for about 1% of people. We're taking a deep dive into the fundamentals of digital marketing for construction companies. These words are for the owner that wants to learn before investing into a digital marketing agency. This is for the construction management student that wants to understand how to market a construction company. I'm writing to the innovative and curious 63-year-old septic company president, who inherited the business from his great-grandfather and is motivated to keep it running and well-branded for future generations. You get the picture. This book is meant to be a tool for the construction industry to gain foundational knowledge of developing a digital marketing strategy.

Before we break ground, I want to take a step back and introduce myself and explain how I ended up writing this book in the first place. My name is Luke Eggebraaten and in 2019, I started my own digital marketing agency called Phaser Marketing. In the years that followed, it evolved to offer digital marketing services *exclusively* to the construction industry. Niching down into construction has allowed our team to add maximum value to our clients by dialing in our systems and processes to a single industry. We don't have to experience the learning curve of a new industry every time we bring on a new client and that has helped us focus our business and work with construction companies all across North America. We have also developed ancillary companies and platforms to cast a wider net and bring more resources into the industry.

We have a sister company, Dirt Work Marketing, which acts as a hyper-specific brand to reach more contractors through social media and website content. You can find us on all social media channels or on our website, dirtworkmarketing.com.

I am also the co-host of the Dirt Bags Podcast with the man, Luke Payne, owner of Black Iron Dirt and Western Excavation. Luke was our very first construction client back in early 2020 and we started the Dirt Bags Podcast together in February 2022 to connect the construction industry and provide valuable resources, content, and referrals from businesses we trust. The podcast has since grown to produce its own educational series: Dirt Bags University. Luke and I have been hosting consistent live webinars for construction owners across the world to network with one another, have a great time, take away something from the speaker, and ultimately learn the way they want to learn. If you want to learn more about the Dirt Bags, check us out on our website, dirtbagspodcast.com.

Additionally, I am an owner of the drag racing company, Turf Wars Racing. I get to be in business with some of my best friends, Jena and Hunter Walz and Jake Sherbrooke, as we bring head-to-head style racing for all ages to events across the country. We see it all on race day; Dirt bikes, quads, side-by-sides, pit bikes, and even the occasional local police cruisers will line'em up for a race. To see more of what we are doing with Turf Wars, follow us on Instagram @officialturfwarsracing or our website turfwarsracing.com.

Separate from the agency, the Dirt Bags, and Turf Wars, I get to collaborate and learn from industry leaders like our friends at BuildWitt, who coined the term "Dirt World". I also get the opportunity to sit on the board of directors for Crew Collaborative, a non-profit with a mission to empower construction's next generation (crewcollab.org). These business ventures, experiences, and (most of all) people inspire me daily and I wouldn't be writing this book without them.

It's important to note that digital marketing is constantly evolving. This is a book, so you can imagine that some of this material will become outdated before I type the last word on my typewriter. However, our focus is on the fundamentals of digital marketing, which will likely remain true for years to come. My hope is this book will be used as a tool, while our website (phasermarketing.com) will provide updated digital marketing trends in construction.

Now, I think it's time we dig into what this book is all about. Thank you from the bottom of my heart for purchasing a copy, even if you don't read it all the way through. It also serves as an excellent drink coaster.

And without further adieu... Let's go!

ONE

YOUR DIGITAL MARKETING PLAN

At first glance, when you consider all the marketing options available in your digital marketing playbook, it might seem overwhelming. This includes your website, search engines (organic, maps, pay-per-click, search engine optimization), social media (Facebook, Instagram, LinkedIn, TikTok), PR Strategy, branding your construction company, and more.

To maximize your online presence, you need to develop a PLAN that covers each of these online marketing opportunities. The purpose of this book is to outline a plan that will transform you from an online marketing newbie to the dominant player in your area.

Throughout this book, we lay the foundation to:

- Map out your online marketing plan
- Start with the fundamentals (Market, Message, Media) before jumping headfirst into your Digital Marketing Strategy
- Set up your website
- Understand how search engines work, and learn the differences between the paid, organic, and map listings

- Optimize with Search Engine Optimization - How to optimize your website with keywords that are most important for your particular business
    - How to conduct keyword research
    - How to optimize your website for ranking in the organic listings on major search engines
    - How to improve your website's visibility so you can rank on page one for your most important keywords
    - Content marketing strategies for maintaining relevance in your market
- Optimize Google Maps - How to get ranked on the Google Map in your area
    - The fundamentals of Google Maps ranking (NAP, Citations, Consistency and Reviews)
    - How to establish a strong name, address, and phone number profile
    - How to properly claim and optimize your Google Business Profile Local Listing
    - How to develop authority for your map listing via citation development
    - List of the top citation sources for your business organization, according to the industry standards
    - How to get real reviews from your clients in your true service area
- Understand Website Conversion Fundamentals - How to ensure that your website converts visitors into conversions
- Understand Mobile Optimization - How to optimize your website for mobile visitors
- Utilize Social Media - How to utilize Social Media (Facebook, Instagram, LinkedIn, TikTok, and other social platforms for maximum effect in construction)
- Understand and capitalize on a public relations strategy

- Use Pay-Per-Click Marketing (Google Ads and Bing Search) - How to maximize the profitability of your Pay-Per-Click Marketing efforts
    - Why PPC should be part of your overall digital marketing strategy
    - Why most PPC campaigns fail
    - How the Google Ads Auction process works
    - How to configure and manage your Pay-Per-Click campaign for maximum Return on Investment (ROI)
- How to track, measure, and quantify your digital marketing plan

When it comes to digital marketing in construction, there are TONS of avenues to explore. In this chapter, we will briefly touch on a couple of channels that are available and being used by other companies, and then go into more detail throughout the book.

This chapter serves as your "Marketing Plan" and roadmap going forward.

Online Marketing Channels

1. Search Engine Optimization (Organic Listings and Map Listings)
2. Search Engine Marketing/PPC on Google Ads and Bing Search Network
3. Social Media Marketing (GBP, Instagram, LinkedIn, TikTok, and Facebook)

Search Engine Optimization

Search Engine Optimization (SEO) is the process of increasing your company's visibility on major search engines (Google, Yahoo, Bing, etc.) in the organic, non-paid listings as consumers are searching for your products or services.

There are three very critical components of Search Engine Marketing. The three components are:

- Paid Listings – The area along the top and side that advertisers can bid on and pay for in order to obtain decent placement in the search engines
- Organic Listings – The area in the body of the Search Engine Results page
- Map Listings – These are the listings which come up beneath the paid listings and above the organic listings in a number of searches

Search Engine Optimization involves getting your website to show up in the Organic and Map Listings. These listings account for a majority of the search volume. More than 78% of searchers click on the Organic (non-paid listings) rather than the paid listings.

When most people think "Digital Marketing," they think Search Engine Optimization. However, you will begin to see that SEO is only a small piece of the MUCH BIGGER "Digital Marketing" puzzle for construction companies.

Search Engine Marketing / Pay-Per-Click

Now that we have discussed SEO, let's talk about Search Engine Marketing or PPC (Pay-Per-Click). Google, Yahoo, and Bing all have paid programs that allow you to BUY listings associated with your keywords to be placed in designated areas of their sites.

There are three really important benefits of PPC:

- Your keyword listings will appear on search engines almost immediately
- You only have to pay when someone actually clicks on your listing – hence the term "Pay-Per-Click"
- You can get your ad to show up on national terms in the areas/cities in which you operate

PPC Marketing works on an Auction system similar to that of eBay. You simply choose your keywords and propose a bid of what you would be willing to pay for each click.

There are several factors that determine placement which will be discussed in detail in the PPC for Businesses chapter. But, in the broadest sense, the one who is willing to pay the most per click will be rewarded the top position in the search engines, while the second-most will be in the second position, etc.

PPC Marketing is a great way to get your company's website to appear at the top of the search engines right away, driving qualified traffic to your website.

Social Media

The big social media channels that we see most utilized in construction are Facebook, Instagram, LinkedIn, and TikTok. Contrary to popular belief, we are seeing a huge wave of the blue-collar industry go online. I always tell people that there is a dirt world cult out on social media and it's not a bad thing. Tons and tons of owners, dozer operators, septic contractors, utility contractors, landscapers and many others are on social media. Their algorithm has their feed dialed in so that they see big iron, construction podcasts, and black excavators on their screen rather than some of the other mindless stuff that's out there. The point is, social media algorithms have become much more advanced to show you what you want to see. I am seeing this have a huge effect for people that appreciate the construction industry.

So, how can you employ these free tools to grow your business? Use it to connect with other construction companies, GCs (general contractors), sub-contractors, your community, potential clients, and most importantly, future employees. By doing so, you can solidify and maintain existing relationships, remain top-of-mind, and brand your business online.

Where to Start?

With such a large amount of digital marketing channels, where should you start? I firmly believe that over time, you should be leveraging each of these online marketing opportunities.

However, you must first begin with the foundation - your website, SEO, and social media. You should start looking at the various paid marketing opportunities *after* your website is set up correctly, ranking on search engines for your most important keywords in the organic, non-paid listings and you are actively engaging in social media activity.

I have found that the biggest and most impactful opportunity is getting ranked organically (in the non-paid listings).

Once you are ranking well organically and things are firing on all cylinders, then you can start to run a well-managed Pay-Per-Click Campaign and continue to increase your online presence.

Throughout this book, we will cover a TON of information. I'm going to mention this now AND at the end. You need to make sure that you are delegating. Do not try and do everything yourself. This book is to help grow your foundational knowledge of what's involved in a digital marketing strategy. I highly recommend that you don't take all of this on yourself, as the quality of execution will be poor AND you will burn yourself out. There are people you can hire, contractors you can bring on, marketing agencies dedicated to construction companies (phasermarketing.com), and tons of resources to assist you so that you don't have to do it all yourself.

In the next chapter, let's take a look at the fundamentals of your overall marketing strategy before pressing forward into full implementation.

TWO

START WITH THE FUNDAMENTALS (MARKET, MESSAGE, MEDIA) BEFORE JUMPING HEADFIRST INTO YOUR DIGITAL MARKETING STRATEGY

Before we dive into Digital Marketing, SEO, PPC and Social Media, I want to be sure we have built a strong marketing foundation.

Let's start with the fundamentals.

So, what do I mean when I say "Fundamentals"? All marketing has 3 core components:

- Message (what)
- Market (who)
- Media (how)

You have to have a unique "Message" (who you are, what you do, what makes you unique, and why someone should hire you rather than another business offering the same service), a specifically defined "Market" (who you sell to and who your best clients are), and then look at "Media" (where you can reach those best clients). The tactics (Pay-Per-Click, SEO, Social Media, Direct Mail, etc.) fall into the "Media" category.

If you focus solely on the Media or Tactics, you will likely fail regardless of how well-selected that Media is. With that being said, you need to scale back to the fundamentals. Invest the time and energy in fleshing out your "Message" and figuring out who your "Market" is. By doing so, ALL of your Media choices will be vastly more effective. How can you do that?

Spend a few minutes and THINK. Take out a scratch pad and answer these questions:

Message:

- What do I do which is unique and different from my competitors? (Do you offer free estimates? Has your company been around for 10 years? 20? 40 years? Do you make it incredibly easy to communicate with you? Will you go out and meet the potential client in-person to do an estimate?)
- If you think about the psychology of a client, what concerns or apprehensions do you think they have about hiring a construction company or sub-contractor? For example, "Will they be able to finish the job on schedule?" or "They are going to be a mess and leave me with more work in the end," or "They are going to give me one price over the phone, tell me another when they start the job, and then charge me something VASTLY different once all is said and done."
- How can you address your clients' common concerns in a unique way? How can you build trust with them before even meeting them?

Market:

- Who is my ideal client? You need to be clear about the audience that you are looking to attract. You may want to target residential homeowners, GCs, home builders, government contracts, city contracts, utilities, septic, bigger construction companies, or maybe even swimming pool companies!
- Look at your last 25 clients and evaluate who spent the most money, who had the highest profit margins, and who was genuinely pleased with your service. What are the unique characteristics of those good clients? Do they live in a particular area of town? Do they have a certain income level? How did they hear about you?
- Start to define who your ideal client is so you can put a marketing plan in place to attract similar clients.

Media:

Once you have fleshed out your Message and your Market, then you can start to think about Media. In order to determine what media will be most effective for you, you need to think about where you can reach your IDEAL client.

Clearly, the Internet is a great "media" for connecting with your ideal client who is proactively in the market for your services. Throughout the remainder of this book, I will explain the various digital marketing channels and how you can use them to connect with your ideal client.

Remember, you need to start with the FUNDAMENTALS (Message, Market, and Media) before running headfirst into any marketing.

THREE

THE BIG ONE: HOW TO SET UP YOUR WEBSITE

This chapter is all about how to set up your website. We are going to cover a lot of details as they relate to SEO, Google Maps Optimization, Pay-Per-Click Marketing, etc.

However, without a properly designed and functioning website, those efforts will be put to waste. Before you can or even should begin exploring those options, you must have an up and running website.

Formats

Let's talk about website formats and the different options available to you when you are ready to start.

1. HTML Site – There are basic HTML (which stands for Hypertext Markup Language, not that you'll ever need to know that) pages and/or individual pages that can be incorporated into a website. This is how almost all websites were built several years ago. They were made up of multiple pages hyper-linked together.
2. Template-Based Site Builders - Site builders, that you can obtain through providers such as Go Daddy, Website Tonight, and 1&1 are turnkey. You

buy your domain and set up your website. I have found this type to be problematic in the long run because you don't have a lot of controller flexibility. But, there are still a lot of sites in this format.
3. CMS Systems - Content Management Systems, like WordPress, Wix, and Squarespace. There are many others, but those are some of the big ones you've likely heard of.

Our agency has worked with all of them, and I would highly recommend going with option 3. A content management system (CMS) is ideal for most businesses due to its scalability. In these platforms, you have the ability to change your navigation on the fly, add as many pages as you need and easily scale out your site.

If you go with option 2 and build your website in a GoDaddy site builder, you are very limited with your scalability and what you can do with the website. Option 1 can also present issues. If you have a fully coded HTML site, it can be incredibly difficult for you to make even the slightest edits, unless you have extensive coding experience.

I always will recommend a CMS, more specifically, WordPress. Everything is built behind code, allowing the ability to apply easy edits and add multiple pages. You can also customize a WordPress website with code if needed.

As you will see in the SEO section of the book, you will have the ability to have a page for each one of your services and each city in which you operate. We will get to that later.

A CMS allows you to create your pages in a scalable format without having to mess around with graphics or do anything that is too difficult to control. It is also easy to access, modify, and update. It is the most popular website format out there.

Using formats like WordPress, you may access the back-end administrative area at *yourcompany.com/login*. After entering your username and password, you will find an easy to edit system with pages and posts which function similarly to Microsoft Word. You can input text, import images and press "save", forcing all new edits to be updated on your live website.

Content Management Systems have intelligently structured links between pages and content, making them extremely search-engine friendly. I have found this method tends to be better than regular HTML or GoDaddy site builder options.

In a lot of cases, a blog is going to be automatically included in a CMS-based website, providing you with a section where you may feed updates. In the SEO chapter, we cover the importance of creating consistent updates and blogging regularly.

Another benefit of using a CMS is the variety of plugins you can choose to incorporate in your website. You can easily pull in your social media feeds, YouTube videos, and Google reviews.

You may also construct your website to automatically post updates to your social media profiles. You can add map integration where people can click to either get directions to your office or view a map to identify the areas served by your organization. There is a surplus of features available within a CMS that are unavailable with a non-CMS option.

Whether you are looking to build a website from the ground up, you are just getting started, or you feel like you simply need a redesign, I highly suggest that you do so in CMS, ideally in WordPress. If you own a construction company and want to take this step but don't know where to start, feel free to reach out to me directly. My team and I get to build construction websites every day and it never gets old.

What Should Your Website Include?

So, which pages does your website need? What navigation structure should you create? Depending on your business, you will need to showcase different things. For most construction companies, the basics include:

1. Home
2. About Us
3. Our Services
4. Our Service Area
5. Reviews and Testimonials
6. Contact Us

These are the core pages. Within "About Us," you might incorporate a drop-down menu for subcategories including "Meet the Team," "Why Choose Us" etc. This set-up can be very powerful because it will deliver everything your website visitor is looking for in a clean and organized fashion.

You want to drive traffic to the "Why Choose Us" section, and, if you are having issues recruiting and retaining good quality talent, you might want to have a "Careers" page under the "About Us" navigation. This is where potential future employees can fill out an application and learn more about your company and culture.

Within "Our Services," you want to have the ability to showcase a drop-down list of the types of services you offer. You want to have landing pages for each one of your services because they are going to be optimized with different keyword combinations. We will discuss this in more depth in the SEO chapter.

Most construction companies have a radius they like to stay within, unless it is a big enough project to make it worth their while. Make sure you highlight these areas on your website and mention which towns, counties, and cities you serve. That way, a visitor can understand right away whether they are a potential client or not. Many commercial clients will still reach out if it is a big enough project and if you have built up enough trust through your website.

A "Reviews and Testimonials" page will provide a section to showcase what your clients are saying about you in text or video form. You can also pull in reviews from sites such as Google Maps, Angie's List, and Yelp. Have a direct link that drives visitors to your online reviews and testimonials. If your business has external credentials, such as being a member of the local chamber of commerce or being BBB-accredited, be sure to include those graphics in the sidebar or header, as well.

Finally, of course, you will need a "Contact Us" page where web visitors have your general contact information. Make it easy for them to enter their information into a web form where they can provide their name, phone number, email address, and a note detailing their requests so they can easily and quickly receive the communication they need.

These core pages make up the foundation of an effective and streamlined website.

A Clear Description of Who You Are

A visitor who stumbles upon your website shouldn't have to do a thorough investigation to figure out who you are and what you do.

This means it's important to clearly mention your business name and sum up your products or services above the scroll section of your website. A clear and specific description that attracts the visitor's attention immediately - within two to three seconds - will encourage them to spend time on your website.

People are most interested in learning about who you are, what you do, and how you can help them. Don't be shy! Tell them your story and the history of your company.

Your Primary Contact Details

Outside of your navigational structure, what else should your website have? What other elements are going to help with conversion?

Well, you should always provide a primary phone number on every page of your website, often in the upper right-hand corner. When somebody visits a page, their eyes are naturally drawn to the top section of the website where they can see the logo and the phone number. It is ideal to make the phone number prominent, telling your visitor to "call now" for service.

An Obvious Call to Action

Construction websites should always make a web form available from which a client can easily request a quote or get more info on how to add you to their bid list.

Remember that every visitor to your website is in a different situation and frame of mind. You may have someone that is looking to contact you for your business services and is willing and able to talk to you immediately.

On the other hand, you also need to consider someone who may not have the ability to stop what they are doing and make a phone call without drawing attention from coworkers. Maybe these visitors are more interested in browsing around to find out what options are available.

Your potential clients may reach your website and be torn between making a call right at that moment, scheduling an appointment, or wanting to have you contact them. Your goal is to provide each of those visitors with the information they need and guide their journey to take action, whether that be filling out a contact form or diving further into your service offerings.

Social Media Links

You also want to provide links to your social media profiles. Link to Facebook, Instagram, LinkedIn, and even your TikTok channel so visitors can easily engage with you on social media, see what you're doing, and follow along with you there. It helps create a sense of authenticity when your clients see your social media content.

Having a social media presence also shows that you are not a one-trick pony. You have a lot of things going on with your business and you are investing into your people, your marketing, your culture, and you have a long-term vision for the future of your company.

Authentic Images

It's extremely important that you infuse personality into your website. The best way to do that is through authentic photos and videos.

Showcase your company, yourself, and the people who work in the business: the office team, the operators, your mechanics, etc.

Showcase the office, the trucks, and the equipment. Use authentic imagery, not stock photography. This gives the visitor the chance to get to know, like, and trust you, before they even pick up the phone. I've seen this tactic prove itself invaluable time and time again.

You must also craft messaging that explains why they should choose your company. Why should someone choose you over the competition?

Guide them down a path where they can start to learn more about why you are their best option. This is where you want to highlight your online reviews and testimonials. For potential clients that are on the fence, this is also where they can quickly locate special offers and incentives that will drive action.

Providing this information will convince site visitors to contact you right away, as opposed to continuing to browse the web for someone else.

Mobile Optimized Website

Another consideration that is crucial to favorable conversion is having a mobile-ready version of your website. More and more people are accessing the Internet with their phones. This shouldn't be a surprise to any of us. Make sure the mobile view of your site isn't a poorly-spaced and tiny version of your desktop site.

It should be intentionally condensed, fitting beautifully on a mobile screen and providing your phone users with just the information they need. It should integrate seamlessly with their phone so all they have to do is press a button to call you.

Those who are searching or accessing your website from a mobile device are often in a different state of mind than the people that are browsing and finding you on a computer. Make it easy for them to get the information they need and get in touch with you.

FOUR

Understanding HOW Search Engines work and the differences between the paid, organic and map listings

In this section, we will take a few minutes to demystify search engines and break down the anatomy of the Search Engine Results Page. By understanding how each component works, you can formulate a strategy to maximize your results.

There are three core components of the Search Engines Results page:

1. **Paid/PPC Listings** – In the paid section of the search engines, you can select keywords relevant to your business and pay to be listed amongst the top search results. The reason it is referred to as PPC or Pay-Per-Click is because rather than paying a flat monthly or daily fee for placement, you pay each time someone clicks on the link.
2. **Map Listings** – The map listings have become very important because they are the first thing that comes up in search results for most localbased searches. If someone searches for a particular service in your area, chances are the map listings will be the first thing they look at. Unlike the paid section of the search engine, you can't buy your way into the Map Listings. You must earn it. Once

you do, there is no per-click cost associated with being in this section of the search engine.
3. **Organic Listings** – The organic/natural section of the Search Engine Results page appears directly beneath the Map Listings in many local searches but appears directly beneath the Paid Listings in the absence of the Map Listings (the Map Section only shows up in specific local searches). Similar to the Map Listings, you can't pay your way into this section of the search engines and there is no per-click cost associated with it.

Now that you understand the three major components of the Search Engine Results and the differences between Paid Listings, Map Listings, and Organic Listings you might wonder... What section is the most important?

The fact is all three components are important, and each should have a place in your digital marketing program because you want to show up as often as possible when someone is searching for your service offerings in your area.

Return On Investment

With that said, assuming you are operating on a limited budget and need to make each marketing dollar count, you need to focus your investment on the sections that are going to drive the strongest ROI.

Research indicates that the vast majority of the population looks directly at the Organic and Map Listings when conducting a search, and their eyes simply glance over the Paid Listings.

So, if you are operating on a limited budget and need to get the best bang for your buck, start by focusing your efforts on the area which gets the most clicks at the lowest cost. We have found placement in the Organic and Map section on the Search Engines drive a SIGNIFICANTLY higher ROI than Pay-Per-Click Marketing (PPC).

Begin with the Organic Listings and then, as you increase your profits, you can start to shift those dollars into a proactive PPC Marketing effort.

In the next chapter, we will take a peek under the hood of Search Engine Optimization and explain how to optimize your website to rank in the organic listings (non-paid) for the most important keywords in your field.

How Do Search Engines Work?

Before we learn how to use search engines to optimize your digital marketing, it isimportant to understand how they work. This includes the process of crawling and indexing, plus the concept of page rank as well.

Search engines work by crawling billions of web pages using their own web crawlers or web spiders. These web crawlers are also known as search engine bots.

Once a webpage is discovered by a search engine bot, it is added into a search engine data structure, a process called indexing. The search engine index includes all the crawled web URLs along with several important key elements about the content of each web URL such as:

- ✔ The keywords
- ✔ Type of content
- ✔ Uniqueness of the page
- ✔ User engagement with the page

Search engine algorithm aims to display a relevant set of high-quality search results that will fulfill the user's search query as quickly as possible.

For example, when someone uses Google to search for the cost for a new septic tank, it is Google's responsibility to connect that person with the best website that is continuing to knock it out of the park. In a nutshell, the search engine's algorithm is the reason your site is either placed toward the top of page one or buried on page 14 where no one will ever find it.

What Happens When a Search Query is Entered?

When a search query is entered into the search engine by a potential user, the search engine tries to identify all the pages which are deemed relevant.

During this process, the search engine uses a special algorithm to hierarchically rank the most relevant pages into a set of results. The algorithm which is used to rank the most relevant web pages differs for each search engine.

For example, a web page that ranks on the top for a search query in Google may not rank highly for the same query in Bing.

Mentioned below are a few elements search engines use to return the results.

- ✔ Search query
- ✔ Location
- ✔ Language detected
- ✔ Previous search history
- ✔ Device from which the search query was entered

Sources and References:

1. https://en.wikipedia.org/wiki/Pay-per-click
2. https://en.wikipedia.org/wiki/Web_crawler

FIVE

SEARCH ENGINE OPTIMIZATION – HOW TO OPTIMIZE YOUR WEBSITE FOR THE KEYWORDS THAT ARE MOST IMPORTANT FOR YOUR CONSTRUCTION COMPANY

You may have heard about SEO, but what does it mean and why is it important for a construction company? SEO stands for Search Engine Optimization, and it is a process of optimizing your website to increase its visibility in search engine results. It is a way of making sure that a website is seen by as many people as possible, and it is an important part of any online marketing strategy.

Think of it this way. If you were to open Google and search, "septic tank installer near me" or "construction jobs in Fargo, ND" or even "what does hydroseeding mean" it is Google's job to match you with the best website to help you out. To clarify, these aren't the pay-per-click Google ads that you see at the top, which are labeled "ad" or "sponsored". When you think about it, when have you ever gone past the first page of Google to find what you're looking for? Typically, you'll click on one of the websites towards the top of the first page that best fits your search. There is a lame digital marketing joke that says if you ever need to hide a dead body, hide it on the 2nd page of Google!

Let's dive in a bit more. SEO is a complex process that involves a variety of techniques and strategies. It involves optimizing not only the content of a website but also its structure and design. It also involves optimizing the website for specific keywords and phrases and for local search engine results. This is typically done by an SEO specialist or a marketing agency. It is very time-consuming but an incredibly powerful skill set for business.

On a simpler note, there are certain things you can do to help your search ranking. Make sure your Google Business Profile (GBP) is verified, accurate, and full of great pictures. It also helps to have detailed descriptions of your services and updates highlighting what you do and who you work with. It is also extremely helpful to get consistent Google reviews on your GBP. Google uses review records as a ranking factor and loves to see consistent 5-star reviews that explain what a great business you are. A great habit that will pay dividends is asking your customers for a 5-star google review and sending them the link directly to their phone. This should be done with every client, GC, board member, sub-contractor, and anyone else that can attest to your character and expertise.

Overall, SEO is an important part of any online marketing strategy for a construction company. By optimizing your website for specific keywords and phrases, local search engine results, social media, and reviews, you can make sure that your website is seen by potential clients who are searching for construction services. This can help you increase your client base and generate more leads, employment applications, and other partnerships.

So now... Let's go a bit deeper.

Getting your company listed in the organic section (non-paid listings) of the search engines comes down to two core factors:

- Having the proper on-page optimization so Google knows what you do and the general area you serve. This allows it to put in the index for the right keywords. You do this by having pages for each of your services and then optimizing them for specific keyword combinations (Ex. Your City + main service, Your City + service 2, Your City + service 3, etc.).
- Creating enough authority and transparency so Google ranks you on page one (rather than page ten) for those specific keywords. Ultimately, it comes down to having credible inbound links and citations from other websites to your website and its sub-pages. He who has the most credible inbound links, citations, and reviews will be the most successful.

There are entire books about SEO so we won't be able to cover it all here, but the goal is to provide you with the actionable fundamentals. Throughout the rest of the chapter, I will provide specific how-to information on exactly what pages to add to a construction website - and why. I also discuss what you can do to improve your authority/transparency in Google's eyes so your website ranks on page one for the keywords most important to your business. These suggestions are catered to a standard excavation/construction company doing 10M or less in revenue. Pages and functions can always be added, but these examples are a good rule of thumb for the bulk of the industry.

Before you start creating pages and trying to do the "on-page optimization" work, you need to be clear on the most commonly searched keywords relative to the services you offer. By understanding the keywords, you can be sure to optimize your website for the words that will drive qualified traffic to your site. One needs to conduct detailed research of the market and the requirements of potential clients in order to find the optimal keywords which will help bring in more clients.

Given that different organizations might be working in different industries, it is imperative to learn the methodology behind selecting the most relevant keywords for your services.

How to Conduct Keyword Research

To determine what your clients are searching for when they need your services, here are several tools that can be used to conduct keyword research. Some are free of charge while others have a monthly cost associated with them. Some of the better keyword research tools include Wordstream, Google Ads Keyword Tool, and SEMRush (Keyword Magic Tool).

For the purpose of this book, we have developed instructions based on the free Google Ads Keyword tool. To use the Google Ads Keyword tool, you'll need to:

- Develop a list of your services and save it in a .txt file

- Develop a list of the cities that you operate in (your primary city of service and the smaller surrounding towns) and save it in a .txt file
- Go to www.mergewords.com
    o Paste your list of cities in column 1
    o Paste your list of services in column 2
    o Press the "Merge!" button
    o The tool will generate a list of all your services combined with your cities of service
- Go to Google.com and search "Google Keyword Planner" or go directly to *https://ads.google.com/home/tools/keyword-planner/*
    o Paste your list of merged keywords into the "word or phrase" box
    o Press "Submit"
- You will now see a list of each of your keywords with a "search volume" number beside it
- Sort the list from greatest to smallest

You now have a list of the most commonly searched keywords in your area.

With this list, you can map out keywords to specific pages on your website and know with confidence you are basing your strategy on opportunity rather than a guesstimate.

How to Optimize for Ranking in the Organic Listings

Step 1 – Build a multi-page website

We have all seen one-page websites before. You know you're on a one-page website when youclick on a menu item and it doesn't take you to a new page, but instead scrolls down the site to the selected section. For many reasons, it's important to build out separate pages and avoid the one-page website. At the very least, you should have a home page, an about page, at least 3-5 individual service pages, a gallery, and a contact page.

For your service pages, build out separate pages for each primary service. For example, if your company does a lot of excavating and grading, create a page with its own content, keywords, FAQ's, photos, and more. Load up each page so that Google sees your site as a resource that can help people get what they're looking (or searching) for.

Step 2 – Optimize Pages for Search Engines:

Once the pages and sub-pages are built for each of your core services, each page needs to be optimized from an SEO perspective in order to make the search engines understand what the page is all about.

Some of the most important items that need to be taken care of for on-page search engine optimization are:

- Unique Title Tag on each page
- H1 Tag restating that Title Tag on each page
- Images named with primary keywords
- URL containing page keyword
- XML Sitemap should be created and submitted to Google Webmaster Tools and Bing Webmaster Tools

How to Build Up Website Authority

Once the pages are built and the "on-page" SEO is complete, the next step is to get inbound links to rank on the first page for your most important keywords.

Everything we have discussed regarding SEO so far lays the groundwork. The website pages need to be well done to even be in the running. However, it is the number of *quality* inbound links and web references to those pages that determines placement.

Building the pages is just the beginning. The only way to get your site to rank above your competition is by having more quality inbound links and citations to your site.

Again, if there is any secret sauce to ranking well in the search engines, it really is links and authority. The major caveat? You can't just use garbage links. You do not want to have a thousand low-quality links. When I say links, I'm referring to other websites hyper-linking to your website, which I'll explain a bit more with specific examples.

A lot of digital marketers and SEO coordinators focus entirely on the quantity of links. Google's algorithm was built upon following links. These digital maketers figured out ways to get a variety of links with random anchor text pointing back to the pages that they want to have ranked. The problem with this method is that Google recognizes that when those links are not relevant, then they don't add any value to the internet.

Bad or irrelevant links can actually hurt your ranking more than help it. It's about getting quality, relevant links back to your home page and subpages through content creation and strategic link-building. How do you get the links? Where do you get the links?

There are a variety of linking opportunities I'd recommend:

Directory Links - There are a number of what I like to call "low-hanging fruit" links.

It all starts with your online directory listings.

Some examples include Google Maps, Yahoo Local, City Search, Yelp.com, Judy's Book, Best of the Web, Yellow Pages, Hot Frog, Service Magic, and the list goes on. All of these online listings let you display your company name, address, phone number, and a link back to your website. Some of them even allow reviews.

For the most part, adding your business information to those directories is completely free of charge. You want to make sure that you have your company listed on as many of the online directory listings as possible for authoritative linking reasons.

They're also valuable from the Google Maps optimization perspective because they provide citations which are very important for getting ranked on the map.

A great way to find additional online directories to add your company to would be to run a search in Google for "Your Company Type – Business Directory" or "Your City – Business Directory". This will give you a great list of potential directory sites to add your company to.

There are also tools for this like BrightLocal or Yext that can provide you with a list of directory sources based on your industry. After beginning with online directory listings, you want to look at any associations you're involved with.

Association Links – Visit the websites of any organizations or associations and get listed in the member section. This will give you citations and the opportunity to link back to your website. Remember, a "backlink" is simply a link to your website on someone else's website.

Non-Competitive Affiliated Industries and Local Businesses - You can get links from GCs, architects, engineers, concrete, framers, or anyone that you work with but don't compete with. It's a great way to collaborate and help each other out. You may create a post on your website about a recent middle school where you did the dirt work. You can highlight the other companies that you worked side by side with to see the project through to completion. You add their logo and a link to their website and show respect for the ones that you have a good relationship with. This is the power of reciprocity. When you do this for others and add value to someone else's business, the benefits will come back your way 10 times over.

Supplier Sites – Look at the suppliers you purchase from and try to coordinate a deal with them. Oftentimes, the places where you buy your materials or products will have a section on their website that mentions their value add resellers. You can get a link from those.

Social Media Profile Links - The other "low-hanging fruit" links are social media profiles. We have a whole chapter about the power of social media and how you can harness it to get repeat and referral business.

Simply from a link-building perspective, you should set up a Facebook page, LinkedIn profile, Google Business Profile, Instagram, TikTok, and a YouTube channel so that you can place a link to your website on each.

All of them will allow you to enter your company's name, address, phone number, description, and, of course, a place to put your website address.

Local Association - Other local associations that you're involved in. If you're a member of the Chamber of Commerce, a networking group like BNI (Business Networking International), or if you're involved with a local charity, find out if they list their members on their websites. Another great place to get links is by typing in your city directory.

Competitive Link Acquisition - The way I like to think of competitive link acquisition is that if quality inbound links are the secret sauce to outranking your competition, and if we can figure out who is linking to your competition or what links your competition have, we can get those same or similar links pointed back to your website. This provides you with more authority and can help you outrank your competitors.

Competitive link acquisition is the process of identifying who is in the top position for your most important keywords, reverse engineering their link profile to see what links they have, and getting those same or similar links pointing back to your website. A simple way to do this is to go to Google and type in "your city + your service," and find out who is in the top few positions.

Let's take a look at the number one placeholder. They are there because their website is optimized well and Google knows they should be ranked well based on the quality and quantity of inbound links compared to the competition.

Once you know who they are, you can use a couple of different tools such as Raven Tools, Majestic SEO, Back Link Watch, etc., to input their URL, run the report, and get a list of links in return.

By analyzing the types of links they have, you can systematically mimic those links and point them back to your website.

Don't just do this for your first competitor, but also for your second, and third, and fourth, and fifth competitors. By doing this on a consistent basis, you can start to dominate the search engines for your most important keywords.

If you build out your site for your services and sub-services, optimize the pages using SEO best practices and then systematically obtain inbound links, you will start to DOMINATE the search engines for your service-related keywords in your area.

Content Marketing Strategies for Maintaining Relevance

Another highly important factor in SEO is maintaining relevance in your market by adding ongoing relevant updates to your website. In the Digital age, content is king.

Google Loves Fresh Content!

In some cases, with the changes in the algorithm, just because you've got a great website with the right title tags and all the best links, you may get discounted if they don't see fresh information posted on a consistent basis.

Google loves fresh content, and it is important to have a methodology in which you are creating and posting content to your website on a regular basis. I want to give you a framework for figuring out what kind of content to write, why you should create content, and how you can do it consistently.

First, you need to understand and accept that you need to be a subject matter expert. You might not consider yourself a writer or a content creator, but you are a subject matter expert.

There are things you know about the dirt world that the general population does not. You're an expert when it comes to the service you are offering, and you have a team of people who are proficient in this area as well. You can create content on the topic that you know most about.

You may not realize it at first, but there are a lot of different topics in your industry to create content about. The most important hurdle you may have is trying to perfect your content. Don't. Let it ride and nerd out about the new septic system you installed, the emergency repair you just did on a sewer line, or why your company uses a tilt rotator. The more you dive below the surface, the more people will trust you as the subject matter expert.

Types of Content

You should also consider that content does not have to be only written words. Content is not just articles. Content can come in a variety of forms. TikTok, Instagram reels, behind-the-scenes footage of your team, and walkarounds of your equipment are just a few of the many ways to produce. As I mentioned earlier in the book, plugging into the different channels and seeing what other contractors are doing can help you get ideas of your own. It's a copy-cat league and the companies starting the trend will take it as a compliment. It will help you get going so that you can create your own original content and have people copying you!

Some people are great writers and that's their strength. Other people like to be on camera. Personally, I think it's a lot easier to create videos because it requires less thinking and more doing.

Managing your expectations is also a crucial part of creating content. Don't expect to make it big on your first one. What matters most is getting regular, creative content out there. The power of consistency will help get you into a positive marketing habit of creating content.

Content Consistency

An effective strategy is to create content on a consistent basis, use the blog on your website as the hub to post it, and then syndicate it to various sources.

You want to syndicate it to article directory sites if it's in text form, and send it to video sites like Vimeo, Metacafe, and YouTube if it's in video form. Doing this keeps the content fresh on your website/domain and creates a lot of authority, which is going to help with the overall ranking of your website on search engines.

You want to make sure you're leveraging each one of these link-building opportunities to maximize your rank potential in your area. You might be surprised that the services you offer are highly competitive from an SEO perspective. There are a lot of companies that want to rank for the same keywords, and many of them have invested heavily in SEO to rank themselves higher in the search engines.

Now that you've built out your website, you've optimized it correctly, and you've got an ongoing link-building and content-development strategy in place, you want to start looking at Google Maps Optimization and getting ranked on Google Maps.

SIX

Google Maps Optimization - How to get ranked on the Google Map in your area

The Fundamentals of Google Maps Ranking (NAP, Citations, Consistency and Reviews)

Getting listed on the first page of Google Maps for "Your City + Service" comes down to four primary factors:

- Having a claimed and verified Google Map Listing
- Having an optimized Google Business Profile listing for the area you operate in
- Having a consistent NAP (Name, Address, Phone Number Profile) across the web so that Google feels confident that you are a legitimate organization located in the place you have listed and serving the market you claim to serve.
- Having reviews from your clients in your service area

If you have each of these four factors working in your favor you will SIGNIFICANTLY improve the probability of ranking on page one of Google Maps in your market.

How to establish a strong Name, Address, Phone Number profile

As I mentioned prior, having a consistent Name, Address, Phone Number (NAP) Profile across the web is essential for ranking well on Google Maps in your area. Google sees it as a signal of authority.

Rather than jumping directly into claiming your Google Map listing and citation-building, it's critical that you start by determining your true NAP so that you can ensure that it is referenced consistently across the web, meaning you want to be certain that you are always referencing the legitimate name for your business.

For example, if your company's name is "Phaser Marketing LLC", you must always list it as "Phaser Marketing LLC," as opposed to just "Phaser Marketing."

The other thing you should be aware of is that there is a lot of misinformation about how to list your company name online. You may read information suggesting that you keyword your name.

For example, if your name is "Tony's Excavating" somebody might tell you it would be really smart if you just added to the title of your company "Tony's Excavating | Excavation in Houston".

While that may have worked back in the day, it's no longer an effective strategy. It's actually a violation of Google Places' policies and procedures.

Make sure you list your exact company name the same way across the board on all your directory sources. Also, make sure that you use the same phone number in all those places. When it comes to your online directory listings, you want to use the primary business phone number you've been using from the beginning.

Don't try to create some unique number for each one of your directories. What that does is confuse your name/address profile. It will hurt you.

Use your primary phone number in all those places, use your exact company name, and use your principal address, written the same way. If your business is located at "2874 North East 94th Street, Suite Number 408," make sure you list it exactly like that every single time.

Don't Forget the Little Details!

Don't neglect to include the suite number in one place and then put it in another. Don't spell out "North East" in one place and put "NE" in the other. We are driving for a consistent name/address profile across the web.

A good way to figure out what Google considers to be your NAP is to run a search on Google for "Your Company" and see what is being referenced on the Google Map.

See how that compares to the other high authority sites like YP.com, Yelp.com, Angie's List, and others. Look for the predominant combination of NAP and reference that for all your directory work going forward. There are many tools that you can use to automatically update your NAP to the directories with one click! Check out BrightLocal, Yext, or SEMRush as they all have listing management features. This is also something that we would help manage as a marketing agency. It's easy for us to do it because we already pay monthly for these tools and software.

How to Properly Claim and Optimize Your Google Business Profile Listing

Below you will find a step-by-step guide for checking, claiming, and managing your Local Business Listings on Google.

1. Go to https://www.google.com/business/

2. Create an Account and claim your business

3. Enter your business address and all pertinent information

4. Choose a verification method

5. Once you've created a profile, go to your Google Business Profile and fill in all the necessary information to optimize your profile.

- Ensure your company name is accurate
- Add your Website Address – This will create an important inbound link
- Upload PHOTOS – AS MANY AS POSSIBLE – Use photos of your equipment, pictures of yourself (the owner), your staff, the office, your trucks, the company logo, and your work. *People Connect and Resonate with images. Leverage that in your Map Listing.*
- Upload a video if you have one (If you don't – make one!)
- List your hours of operation and services offered

Optimize your Google Business Profile Listing

You'll manage your business listing from your Google Business Profile. This is where you'll make changes to your company information and gain insights into how popular your business is by seeing how many times your profile has been viewed on Google Maps.

There are a number of Best Practices you need to be aware of to properly optimize your Map listing.

- *Company Name* – As mentioned before, always use your legal business name – don't cram additional words into the name field. Ex. If your company name is "Johnson Construction" don't try to put additional keywords like "Johnson Construction - Detroit". This would be against the Google Places guidelines and will reduce your probability of ranking.
- *Address* – On the "Address Field" use your EXACT legal address. You want to ensure that you have the same address listed on your Google Places listing as it is on all the other online directory listings like CitySearch.com, YellowPages.com, Yelp.com, etc. The consistency of your NAP (Name, Address, Phone Number Profile) is very important for placement.
- *Phone Number* – Use a local number (not an 800 number), and make sure it is your real office number rather than a tracking number. We find that 800 numbers don't rank well. If you use a tracking number, it won't be consistent with your other online directory listings and will result in poor ranking.
- *Categories* – You can use up to five categories, so use ALL five. Be sure to use categories that

describe what your business "is" rather than what it "does". So, you would use "Construction Company" rather than "grading services" The latter would be considered a violation of Google's regulations and would hurt rather than help you.

- Service Area and location settings – Google offers two options here:

    1. No, all customers come to my location
    2. Yes, I serve customers at their location

If you own a construction company and don't have an office or a shop, you would likely need to select "Yes, I serve..." because you and your team are typically visiting the clients on site. Not doing so can result in a penalty on your listing. On the other hand, if you have a shop or an office, you could show this address and in this case, you would likely choose "No, all customers...".

- The next option is "Do not show my address". You can choose this if you do not want your address shown. Keep in mind, it is much tougher to rank in your local area without a business address on your Google Business Profile and Google Map listing.

- If you don't have a business address or a home address to list, the only other option is a virtual office. Unfortunately, P.O. Box addresses and mailboxes don't tend to rank well.

- Picture and Video Settings – You can upload up to ten pictures and five videos. Use this opportunity to upload authentic and quality content about your company. It's always best to use real photos of your team, office, and equipment rather than stock photos.

- Pictures – You can get more juice from this section by saving the images to your hard drive with a naming convention like "your city + excavation contractor – your company name," rather than the standard file name. You can also create geo context for the photos by uploading them to a video-sharing site like Panoramio.com (a Google Property) that enables you to Geo Tag your photos to your company's location.

- Videos – Upload VIDEOS. They don't have to be professionally produced and will resonate well with your clients. A best practice is to upload the videos to YouTube and then Geo Tag them using the advanced settings.

Once you have optimized your listing using the best practices referenced above, you want to be sure that you don't have any duplicate listings on Google Maps.

Duplicate Listings

We have found that even just one or two duplicates can prevent your listing from ranking on page one. In order to identify and merge duplicate listings, run a search on Google for "Company Name, City".

To clean up duplicates, click on the listing in question and then click "edit business details."

- Click "This is a duplicate" to let Google know that the listing should be merged with your primary listing.

If you follow these best practices, you will have a well-optimized Google Maps listing for your company!

How to Develop Authority for your Map Listing via Citation Development

Now that you have claimed your Google Business Profile Listing and optimized it to its fullest, you need to build authority.

Having a well-claimed and optimized local listing doesn't automatically rank you on page one. Google wants to list the most legitimate and qualified providers first. So, how do they figure out who gets a page-one listing?

Well, there are a number of determining factors, but one of them is how widely the company is referenced on various online directory sites such as Yellow Pages, City Search, Yelp, and others.

Citations are web references to your company name, address, and phone number (NAP). You can add citations in a variety of ways. There are directory listings that you should claim manually and others that you can submit to via submission services like Universal Business Listing or Yext.com.

TOP Citation Sources to Claim Manually:

- Google Business Profile
- Bing Local
- Yahoo Local
- City Search
- FourSquare.com
- Yelp
- YP.com
- Merchant Circle
- Manta

List of the Top Citation Sources for Businesses

1) **Google**

Google is probably the most important and most talked about place to list your local business. Getting citations from many of the sites below (as well as ratings) can help boost your business listing on Google.

2) **Yelp**

One of the most popular social networking, directory, and review site that many of us don't enjoy. Aside from counting as a citation for your business in the eyes of major search engines, this site can deliver quite a bit of traffic on its own. However, business owners using Yelp will need to learn to deal with the occasional nasty review and their brutal sales calls.

3) **Foursquare**

A popular way to check in to various locations using a smartphone. This can also provide a valuable citation for your local business.

4) Universal Business Listing

A local listing service – UBL.org (along with Localeze below) is one of the major players in the effort to only fill in your information once while getting listed on multiple yellow pages sites, directories, and social networking/review sites. It saves time and effort but may be slower than going directly with the individual sites (see Localeze and InfoUSA below).

5) Yahoo Local

Yahoo's Local directory is tied to Yahoo Maps.

6) Local.com

Business listings, event listings, coupons, and reviews

7) CitySearch

One of the most authoritative local directories

8) Bing Local

Bing's local business listing service is integrated with maps of cities and towns.

9) Craigslist

Some recommend creating classifieds for your business on popular sites such as Craigslist. There's some disagreement over whether this is effective from an SEO point of view.

10) GetListed.org

A convenient way to identify where you are and are not listed in major directories. Provides referrals to Universal Business Listings and Localeze as well as consultants (if you need extra help).

11) **DMOZ (Open Directory Project)**

A free and authoritative index (in the eyes of Google) that is managed by volunteers.

If you can get your business listed, this helps with an authoritative backlink (but not necessarily a local citation). It can be difficult to get a new listing due to the limited resources and large volumes of submissions.

12) **Superpages**

One of the many Internet Yellow Pages directories (IYP). Includes business listings, people search, reviews, and local deals.

13) **Localeze**

A multiple local listing service

14) **InfoUSA**

A multiple local listing service

15) **Your local Chamber of Commerce**

Joining your local chamber of commerce can often get you a business listing (and a citation for local SEO purposes)

16) **InsiderPages**

Local directory and rating site

17) **Merchant Circle**

Local directory and rating site

18) **Best of the Web**

A popular directory with free and paid listing options – specifically for local, they have a Best of the Web Local directory.

19) **Yellowpages.com**

Internet yellow pages (also YP.com)

20) **Judy's Book**

Social search and online yellow pages

21) **Business.com**

Business.com provides business information but also has a business directory.

22) **Better Business Bureau**

Your local Better Business Bureaus will usually charge for membership and provide a link to your business.

23) **DexKnows**

Business and people directory

24) **Your local newspaper's website**

Getting an article, business listing or classified ad optimized with your local information and a link can provide a citation for your business.

25) **HotFrog**

A business directory with free and fairly inexpensive paid listing options.

26) **Crunchbase**

A listing of technology companies that is user generated.

27) **Angie's List**

Service provider directory

28) **Jigsaw**

Businesspeople and company directory

29) **iBegin**

US and Canadian business directory

30) **Wikimapia**

Wiki-based directory of places including schools, businesses, and more – laid out on maps.

31) **CitySquares**

Local business directory with ratings

32) **InfoSpace**

Business and people listings

33) **MagicYellow**

A straightforward Internet yellow pages directory

34) **Whitepages.com**

People and business listings

35) **Manta**

Company profiles

36) **EZLocal**

Local business listings and ratings

37) **BrownBook**

Local business listings and ratings

38) **CityVoter**

Vote for favorite businesses

39) **ShopCity**

Local business listings

40) **YellowBot**

Local listings and ratings

41) **MojoPages**

Social networking and review site (like Yelp)

42) **Tupalo.com**

International social networking and review site

43) **GetFave**

Business directory, including featured listings (with additional content such as videos and pictures)

44) **BizJournals**

Business journal that includes business directories for certain US cities

45) **Tjoos**

Online store listings and coupons

46) **JoeAnt**

Website directory

47) **Zidster**

Products, services, or business listings

48) **TrueLocal**

Business directory – seems to have sparse listings

49) **ZipLeaf**

Network of international business directories

50) **WCities**

Places and events for cities and towns, including ratings.

51) **Naymz**

Personal branding site

52) **ZoomInfo**

Database of people and companies

53) **Yellowikis**

Wiki-based business directory

54) **GoMyLocal**

Yellow pages/local directory

55) **Fast Pitch Network**

Online business networking site

56) **City Slick**

Free business directory

57) **yellowpages.lycos.com**

A general directory

58) **Home Advisor**

Directory of service companies (includes a "seal of approval")

By securing these high-quality citations, you will boost your authority and highly improve your probability of ranking in Google Maps Listings. The next critical step is to get online reviews.

How to Get Online Reviews: Real Reviews from your Real Clients in your True Service Area

The next critical component for getting ranked on Google Maps, after you've claimed and optimized your listing, established your NAP, and developed your citations across the web, is obtaining reviews. You need to have real reviews from your real clients in your true service area.

Keep it Real

First, I want to point out that you shouldn't fill the system with fake reviews. You do not want to create bogus accounts and post reviews to Google Maps, Yelp, City Search, etc. just for the sake of saying you've got reviews. That's not going to help you. You need real reviews from your actual clients in your true service area.

You might be thinking "Well, why is that important?" or "How would Google know the difference?" Google is paying very close attention to the reviewer's profile.

If somebody is an active Google user, their profile is likely connected to Gmail account and a YouTube channel. Say that person with the active profile has had their account for seven years and actually happens to be located in your service area. If he or she writes you a review, it would be considered credible and will count in your favor.

Now, if somebody creates a Google account with the sole intent of writing a review, Google is capable of catching on to that. If that account has no history associated with it and it originated from your office IP address, that review is going to be flagged as a bogus submission.

It is important to have an authentic strategy in which you are connecting with real people who will write your reviews. You don't want to try and play the system. Google and other popular review sites are fully aware of the games played by businesses and they have created products to weed out the inauthentic.

Getting Reviews

With that said, how can you get reviews? What kind of process do you need to actually get reviews from your real clients in your real service area? Here's the strategy we recommend:

First of all, print some review cards. These are simple documents with your company logo and a short thank you note while asking for a review. You can even create a free QR code with a direct link to leave a review on your google listing.

Here's an example of what you can write on your review cards: "Thank you so much for being a trusted client! We appreciate the opportunity to take on all of your site work needs. If you could take a few minutes to write us a review, that would help us a ton!" Then give them a link to a page on your website or the QR code where they can write you a review.

You will want to do some homework on the front end. Be sure you have a page on your website that is clearly meant for reviews (yourcompany.com/reviews). On that page, you want to include links to places where customers can write your reviews.

I always recommend that you lead with getting Google reviews. Don't worry too much about getting all the other reviews on different platforms. They certainly help, but the Google reviews will hold the most weight.

The next step is to develop an email list of your circle of influence, which gives a nice bump in the number of reviews you have. Your circle of influence is going to be your most recent clients, the clients who have been using your services for quite some time, your family members, and your friends. People that you know, like, and trust, and who would be willing to vouch for you.

Put together that email list in an Excel sheet. It might be

10 contacts, or it might be 700. Then, use a tool like Constant Contact, MailChimp, or another email marketing tool to send an email blast with the following message:

Email Subject: Thanks for your business!

Name,

I wanted to shoot you a quick email to thank you for your business and let you know how much we appreciate the opportunity to take on your project!

Our goal is to provide 100% client satisfaction and exceed your expectations every step of the way. I certainly hope that we did just that!

If so, it would really help us out if you'd be willing to post a review for us online at one of your favorite online review sites. Below are a few sample direct links where you could write a public review about your experience with us:

- **Google** - (Toss the link to your GBP in here)
- **Facebook** - (Link to your FB Recommendation section here)

Thank you again! We really appreciate your support!

All the best,

Luke Eggebraaten

Make sure you save them the time of having to find the websites on their own by providing some links to the various places where they can write reviews.

By sending this email, you're going to increase your online review profiles and jumpstart your Google-approved authenticity as a business. Getting the first ten reviews on Google Maps is essential.

It makes a huge difference in how you rank, and it gives you a different perception in the mind of your customers. You want to get past that ten review threshold almost immediately.

Doing that helps you get real reviews from real people that have real online profiles. Again, you want to have a systematic process in place where you are asking for reviews on a consistent basis from the clients that you are serving on a daily basis. The best way to do that is to request an email address from your clients, either at the point of service or after service.

If you follow these steps to properly claim your Google Map listing, develop your authority via citation development, and put a systematic process in place to get real reviews from your real clients in your true service area, you will be well on your way to dominating the Google Map listings in your market.

SEVEN

WEBSITE CONVERSIONS - HOW TO ENSURE THAT YOUR WEBSITE CONVERTS VISITORS

This chapter is all about website conversion fundamentals. We talk about how you need to set up your website, the messaging on your website and the navigational flow to ensure maximum conversions. You may be looking to hire and attract talent, convert a GC by having them click to call you, or even a company that's impressed with your work and wants to set up a brand deal with you.

The way I look at it is, you can have the best Pay-Per-Click campaign, Search Engine Optimization, and be ranked number one on Google Maps, but if the content and the structure of your website isn't set up in a way that's compelling for visitors, then it doesn't give them a reason to choose you over someone else. It doesn't give them the information that they need to easily say, "You're the company that I am going to call." If your website doesn't convert customers, all your effort to drive traffic to your site will be useless. Make sure that your website represents your company well and makes an impact on anyone looking at it.

I want to talk about how we can take the traffic we're

going to get from organic and Pay-Per-Click strategies and make sure that the website is illustrating the correct message so we can maximize the profitability and revenue of our online marketing strategies.

Conversion Fundamentals

Be real. I talked about how people resonate with real people. They like to see the company, the people that they are going to be talking with on the phone, and that are going to be going out to their home. So, as often as you can, avoid stock photography. Get a picture of the owner, the team, your office, your equipment, anything to make it feel personable.

These things really draw people in and help them feel that they would be working with real people. That is the kind of business that people want to deal with. People want to work with people. Yes, I did just say people 5 times.

As for the content of your website, write messaging that draws them in and makes them connect. They're looking for a utility contractor, excavation company, or landscaping contractor, so when they land on your home page, the first message they see should enforce the fact that they can trust you.

Connect with them. Give them reasons to choose you and have a call to action, "24/7 emergency water line repairs" or, "Click here to receive an estimate on your next job". Having multiple Calls to Action (CTAs) to click as they're browsing your website will help increase your conversion rate, no matter what your goal is.

What to Write

When it comes to the copy or messaging, on the website, you want to address their specific concerns.

For example, if you own a small excavation outfit, help educate visitors on what you do, how you make GCs lives a bit better, what your company values are, and answer all FAQs that people may have!

Write that kind of messaging for each one of the pages on your website including a clear CTA after every block of text saying, "Call now" or "Click here to get started".

Pull them deeper into your website with "About Us" links, past jobs, and links to before and after images.

Give them content that makes them think, "These guys know what they're doing," and draw them deeper and deeper into the website so they're more inclined to take the next step. Explain what makes you so special and why you are still in business today.

You should also, of course, have a web form on each of the pages of your website or, at a minimum, on the "Contact Us" page. Make sure your site features accessible ways to get ahold of you. Not everyone wants to fill out a contact form, so seeing that there is an easy call now button will help with your conversion. I definitely recommend having a lead form, a hiring or application form, and an accessible CTA with your phone number.

Explain why they should choose you. Leverage personality. Be authentic. Integrate your photos into your website. I can't stress this enough: personal, genuine, authentic content really helps with conversion.

Utilize your reviews, testimonials, and videos. There's no reason you can't create a simple video for each of the pages on your website, explaining what the service is, and why your business can do it best. Some customers are visual so they may be fine reading the content on the website. Other people are more audible and would prefer to hear the message.

Show them what other people are saying, and you're going to significantly improve your conversion. Be real and transparent, and show some of your personality on your website. What makes you different from all the other companies out there? Get creative, you don't need to follow a script.

EIGHT

MOBILE OPTIMIZATION - HOW TO OPTIMIZE YOUR WEBSITE FOR MOBILE USERS (BASICALLY EVERYONE)

It's no secret. MOST people have a phone that has internet access. We all have this powerful computer in our pockets that we use for everything and anything.

We have all been there. We search for a company real quick, go to their website, and it is super zoomed out or cut off. If a site is not optimized for mobile, it will not only scare off the few people that end up on the site, but Google will identify that website as one they don't want to send ANYONE to. Let's get that fixed ASAP.

Mobile-Optimized Websites

Go find some websites in your industry that you love. You can find an entire portfolio of mobile-optimized construction websites at phasermarketing.com or reach out to me and I can send you some of our favorites. It's always a good idea to see what others are doing to inspire your vision of what you want your website to look like.

Analyze Your Mobile Status

Many business owners pump a lot of muscle into competing with similar businesses while neglecting to take a close look at what they're doing. Analyzing your mobile status will help you figure out which weaknesses are holding you back and which strong points can help you win the war.

You need to understand where your past efforts have taken you, as well as what your future has in store for you based on where you stand today.

Ask yourself the following:

- When you look at your website on mobile, is it user-friendly? Does it load within seconds or take forever to render properly? Does your mobile website have all the relevant information on it that consumers look for while on the go?
- Does your mobile website come up high in the rankings on mobile search engines, or is it nowhere to be found when local consumers perform a search for your "service + your city" on their phone?
- Is your opt-in/call-to-action on all of your printed and marketing materials?
- Are you using QR codes as an additional method of increasing awareness about your company? Do you have your QR codes on all your other marketing materials? Are you using them to direct traffic to your website?

As you can see, there are a lot of things to consider when it comes to making sure your company is on the right track toward excelling online in your community and an example for other construction companies to follow across the country.

Make Clients Call Your Business with Mobile Marketing

How can you make your company more interesting to your target audience?

It is up to you which tools you leverage to attract and retain attention, employees, and clients. Your main focus should be geared toward adding value to the visitors on your site. Don't spend all your time worrying about competition. Go fix your business and stay focused on how you can improve.

Here are a few tips which can work in your favor and help:

- You need to have a good website that is mobile-friendly and easily accessible by mobile phone users in your area. People are using their mobile phones to access the web to search for local products and services while on the go. Make sure your site loads quickly, provides the information your customers need, and is easy to navigate.

- If you choose to start an SMS marketing campaign, make sure your texts offer great value, relay a clear message, and are short and informative. Also, be sure to send messages out consistently, yet conservatively. Create a careful balance that makes sense for your business and your target audience. Need a boost in getting new mobile subscribers? Give your clients and prospects a great incentive in exchange for opting in and watch your list grow exponentially.

- Consumers and future employees love businesses that stay "on top" of the digital age. They expect you to have a website, be actively involved in their favorite social media outlets, be an active member of the community, and be easily accessible from their mobile devices.

- Mobile SEO should be used effectively to attract qualified traffic to your website. Mobile users search for local products and services constantly on their mobile devices when on the go. If your business does not rank in the results, there is a major potential profit leak left for your competitors to scoop up (Tony's Excavation is coming in hot).

NINE

Social Media Marketing
How to leverage Social Media (Facebook, Instagram, LinkedIn & TikTok)

Social Media Strategies for Construction Companies

Modern construction companies are discovering the importance of social media and its potential to expand their reach, build brand awareness, and ultimately drive leads and sales. As more people turn to social media for both personal use and business purposes, it is essential for construction companies to understand how to leverage this powerful marketing medium in order to succeed. In this chapter, we'll dive into some key tips for developing an effective social media strategy for construction companies.

Analyze Your Audience

The first step in any successful social media strategy is understanding who your target audience is and where they hang out online. Take time to research what platforms they are using, what kind of content they engage with, and how often they interact with brands. It's also a good idea to take a look at what your competitors are doing on social media so you can find inspiration and develop ideas that will resonate with your own followers.

Choose The Right Platforms

Once you have identified your target audience, it's important to choose the right platforms based on their preferences. If your goal is to reach industry professionals, LinkedIn might be the best option while Instagram or YouTube could be great choices if you're looking to connect with a younger demographic. Additionally, consider mixing up the type of content you post across different networks as each platform has its own unique features that you can use effectively to engage with your followers.

Craft Engaging Content

Creating content that resonates with your audience is key when it comes to establishing an effective social media presence. Make sure all posts have a clear purpose, whether it's driving website traffic or creating brand awareness, and consider using visuals such as videos or images whenever possible as these tend to perform better than text-based updates. Additionally, remember the power of storytelling; incorporating stories into your posts will help keep people engaged and create deeper connections with them over time.

Monitor And Measure Performance

Finally, monitor performance regularly by tracking likes, comments, shares, etc. This will help you determine which types of content produce the best results so you can focus on creating more of that kind in the future. Additionally measuring KPIs such as website visits from social sources will give a better indication of which campaigns are driving ROI. By closely monitoring data, you'll gain valuable insight into what works well (and what doesn't) so that you can make adjustments accordingly in order to maximize performance going forward.

Social media offers a powerful tool that is completely free and can be a game-changer for connecting with other construction companies, contractors, potential clients, future employees, and your community. Developing an effective strategy requires you to post. That's it. Step 1, you need to start posting. Creating. Engaging. Social media is meant to be social. Don't overthink it, add value, show some cool equipment, nerd out about the septic system you're installing, comment on other businesses' posts, and don't be so rigid. Do some research on your target audience and see who's engaging with your content on each platform.

The Basics: How to Set Up a Facebook Company Page & Ads Account

Creating a presence on social media is an important part of any construction company's marketing strategy - and setting up a page on Facebook can be the perfect way to reach potential clients. Here are some steps on how to do just that:

Create a Page

The first thing you need to do is create a page where you will post updates and information related to your business. To get started, head over to facebook.com/pages and click "Create Page" at the top right corner of the screen. Fill out all relevant information about your company and add a profile picture before clicking save at the bottom of the page; this will be visible to users when they visit your page.

Customize & Optimize

Once created, it's time to customize your page with extra features such as creating tabs for specific topics (e.g. "Construction Services" or "Portfolio"). You should also take advantage of local optimization opportunities by adding relevant contact information, opening times, etc. Additionally, make sure all visuals used are in line with brand guidelines and formatted appropriately so they look good when displayed on the page itself; don't forget to create cover images too!

Set Up Ads Account

To promote your new Facebook page or advertise other services, it's necessary to set up an ads account which can be done by logging into facebook.com/business with your existing credentials and following the instructions provided there regarding payment details, etc. Once everything is set up correctly, select "Ads Manager" from the left-hand menu which will give you access to all campaign-related features such as ad creation, budgeting options, and much more.

Creating a Facebook company page and setting up an ads account may seem like daunting tasks but both are relatively easy once you get started. Having access to these tools can help any business increase its online presence and spread awareness about its services more effectively.

How Meta Connects Your Instagram & Facebook Company Profiles

You may have noticed that Facebook has made some big changes over the last couple of years. One of the biggest is the name change to Meta, and how they are connecting your Instagram and Facebook company profiles. This integration allows users to access insights regarding both channels, carry out competitive analysis, and compare engagement rates in order to get a better understanding of the state of their digital marketing campaigns. Moreover, with Meta's integrated calendar view, companies can plan and schedule content across multiple platforms quickly and efficiently. Here are some of the key advantages of connecting your Instagram & Facebook company profiles:

Increased Visibility

Connecting your accounts makes it easier for followers to find your content on multiple platforms with just one click. Additionally, cross-promoting posts can help increase visibility by reaching audiences that may have not yet been reached before due to different interests among different groups. This increases brand recognition and gives construction companies more exposure online which can lead to more leads and conversions!

More Efficient Scheduling

Many construction companies struggle to keep up with social media schedules as posting too frequently or not often enough can lead to missed opportunities or oversaturation of content. However, having all accounts connected under one platform reduces this issue significantly. With Meta's integrated calendar view, users can easily visualize upcoming content trends over multiple weeks and manage postings more effectively.

Access To Insights & Metrics

Once your accounts are linked up, you'll be able to see exactly how much engagement each post is receiving on both platforms in real-time. This makes it easier for construction businesses to identify what works (and doesn't work) when it comes to their social media presence so they can make adjustments if needed. Additionally, having unified analytics data makes tracking progress against objectives such as increasing website traffic or boosting followings much easier than ever before. Connecting Instagram & Facebook Company profiles is an effective way for construction companies to increase their online visibility while making sure they remain on top of social media scheduling demands - and Meta is a great solution.

How to Set Up and Manage a LinkedIn Company Profile for a Construction Company

LinkedIn is an *invaluable* tool for construction companies to grow their brand and for you as an individual to build your network, grow your business, and make a huge impact. More on that in a few pages. First, I want to give you the steps on how to create and manage a successful LinkedIn company profile:

Create Your Page

The first step is to create your company page - head over to business.linkedin.com/marketing-solutions/company-pages/getting-started and click "Create" at the top of the page. Fill out all of the necessary information before clicking save at the bottom of the page; this will be visible to users when they visit your page so it's important to make sure everything is correct. All company pages must be connected to an admin, which would likely be you. I see this as a positive because it will help motivate you to get your personal page up and going as well.

Customize & Optimize

Once created, make sure you customize your page with features such as adding links to other platforms, creating tabs for specific topics (e.g. Construction services, portfolios, past projects, hiring events, your website, your crew), and adding relevant contact information. Additionally, make sure all visuals used are in line with brand guidelines and formatted appropriately so they look good when displayed on the page itself; don't forget to create a sweet cover image too!

Develop & Post Content

Developing content for your company profile is essential if you want to stand out and get on LinkedIn's good side. Aim for high-quality posts which add value for readers such as useful tips about construction practices or industry news that might be of interest. We also see successful pages that dive deep into their projects their currently on, *why* they are doing what they're doing, what equipment they're using for the job, and how this is important. Be yourself and do your best to add value to your network. Be the subject matter expert.

Also, don't be afraid to tag yourself, and make sure to tag other partners, suppliers, GCs, clients, and anyone else that would make sense to be mentioned in the post. Give them a shoutout for being on-time and awesome to work with. Show them some true appreciation and let your network know about it. This will typically be followed with a re-share on their company page, which then extends your brand out to multiple networks that you haven't reached yet.

Creating a successful LinkedIn company profile requires careful planning and the willingness to put yourself out there, but can pay dividends if done correctly. Following these steps should set you off on the right path toward achieving LinkedIn domination.

In my opinion, every construction company should be active on the Big 3 (FB, Insta, and LinkedIn) with TikTok being an optional 4th round draft pick. Cross-posting onto your Google Business Profile and utilizing that as an additional social media channel will have a huge positive effect on your SEO and people finding you.

Here's a hint of who you are likely going to be engaging with on each platform:

Instagram: Great for connecting with other construction companies all over the world. The Dirt World has a ton of these companies and Instagram is one of the best to network with others that may be experiencing some of the same things you're going through. Get on there and start following and engaging with others to build up a network that you can rely on.

Facebook: No matter what your feelings are toward Facebook, you should definitely have one for your business. Get it set up and make sure you start joining Facebook groups! We see a lot of exposure and leads come through Facebook. It's an easy one to get set up and can be very powerful for many reasons. When you get to a point where you want to run Facebook ads, it's a lot easier to do it with a company page that is built up and has a solid reputation.

TikTok: This one is always great because if you're not on the app, you think it's a bunch of BS and people dancing. However, there is an entire construction community on the platform and it is extremely valuable if you can get your algorithm tuned to your liking. Many contractors are on the platform to learn, see some sweet videos, new equipment, how-to's on certain services, construction business advice, and a lot more. I would compare it to a similar audience as Instagram. You are going to get to meet a lot of other contractors that are in the same boat as you, as well as smaller and larger construction companies.

LinkedIn: You've heard me say it before and I will continue saying it. LinkedIn is where it's at. The ratio of LinkedIn users that create compared to the users that consume is way out of whack. Simply put, there are more people watching on LinkedIn and not enough creating. You can easily add value and build your personal/company brand on the platform. It's a bonus that when someone is on the app, it is typically to learn something, network, get a job, or do some business. It has the highest ratio of presidents, CEOs, and decision-makers out of any social media platform. If you apply one thing from this book, it would be to start creating and posting on LinkedIn. Go get it done. Also, if you got this far in the book, shoot me a LinkedIn message so that I can keep an eye on the progress of your account. I'm pumped to see the network you are going to build up!

TEN

Public Relations (PR) in construction

A PR strategy is a plan of action that outlines how a company will use public relations to achieve its goals. It is a comprehensive plan that outlines the company's objectives, target audience, messaging, tactics, and budget. A PR strategy can benefit a construction company in a variety of ways:

First, a PR strategy can help a construction company build its brand and reputation. By creating a positive image in the public eye, a construction company can attract more clients and increase its visibility. A PR strategy can also help a construction company stay ahead of the competition and on top of the minds of future employees by keeping up with industry trends and news.

Second, a PR strategy can help a construction company build relationships with key stakeholders, such as clients, suppliers, and partners. By engaging with these stakeholders, a construction company can build trust and loyalty, which can lead to increased sales, referrals, and recognition.

Third, a PR strategy can help a construction company manage its reputation in the event of a crisis. By having a plan in place, a construction company can respond quickly and effectively to any negative publicity or criticism.

Finally, a PR strategy can help a construction company reach new audiences. By leveraging the power of social media, a construction company can reach a wider audience and increase its visibility.

PR has been around for centuries, but its modern definition comes from PR pioneer Edward Bernays who described PR as "the engineering of consent". PR is now considered an essential component of any digital marketing strategy and a PR plan can help construction companies build strong relationships with their clients, community, and media. It is also a great way to pour some more gas on your online presence. Here are 20 tips broken up for a construction company to develop an effective PR plan that will raise its presence and give them the edge in the competitive world of construction.

1. Set Clear Objectives – Establishing PR goals and objectives is key to developing an effective PR plan. Think about what you want to achieve, such as increased visibility, more trust within your local community, national coverage, or more favorable perceptions of your company. You want your objectives to be clear. What are we trying to accomplish here?

2. Research Your Audience – Who are you trying to reach? Why are you trying to reach them? What channels do they use for communication? How does your audience currently perceive your brand? Do they even know about you? Knowing your target audience is essential for PR campaigns that are tailored to their needs. Give the people value and something eye-catching.

3. Develop a PR Strategy – Once you know your objectives and your target audience, it's time to develop a PR strategy that will help you reach them. Consider the most effective methods of communication for reaching each segment of your audience, such as online or traditional outreach. The following tips will help you put together an all-around strategy. Don't expect a PR strategy to solve all of your problems. This is just a piece of your overall digital marketing strategy. You want to make sure that you've got all other elements dialed in and continue to improve them as you go.

4. Define Your Message – Knowing what you want to say and how to say it is huge for success. Make sure your messaging reflects the values, principles, history, and legacy of your business. If your construction company was started by your grandfather and passed down for generations, make sure you convey the message of your company's history and how you have taken care of your clients for X amount of years. Dial in your message and how you want it to come off as people are reading it.

5. Connect with Key Influencers – There are tons of solid influencers in the dirt world. Many of them may not even realize it or consider themselves an "influencers". It's certainly a term that we don't think about in the construction space but they are definitely out there! Find leaders in the industry who are active on LinkedIn, have a podcast, are a leader at your local chamber of commerce, have tons of Instagram followers, are exhibiting or

speaking at tradeshows, or even someone that seems to be in the local newspaper every month with the work they are doing in the community. Do your best to connect with these influencers and get to know them. Ask them questions about their business and their passions. Be interested in *them*, and it will come back your way.

6. Invest in a PR Firm – PR firms can be a valuable asset for construction companies looking to execute PR plans, as they possess the tools and expertise necessary for success. However, I typically wouldn't recommend anyone that's doing less than 2M in yearly revenue to invest in a PR firm. A lot of this can be bootstrapped or contracted out until your brand and team are big enough to sustain the cost.

7. Monitor Your Progress – Keep track of metrics like website traffic and social media engagement to see how successful your PR efforts are. This can help you make adjustments where needed. Make sure you can tell the difference between what is coming from the PR and what is coming from other digital marketing channels. You can see this information in your analytics tracking.

8. Leverage PR Opportunities – Keep an eye out for PR opportunities, such as awards or speaking engagements, that may be beneficial to your whole strategy. Lead with adding value at tradeshows, luncheons, fundraisers, and conferences. Make sure the event managers know you're available and trust you to take care of their event as a speaker. This can be a great way to get up on stage and is a huge factor in your PR performance.

9. Have a Digital Presence – A strong online presence is essential for PR success in the digital age, so focus on creating and maintaining an up-to-date website and engaging regularly on social media. If only there was a book that dove into these elements a bit more. Could be called *The Digital Dirt World*, or something along those lines.

10. Remain Professional – Always strive for professionalism in PR efforts, as this will help you build trust with your clients and stakeholders. Don't act desperate. As I mentioned before, lead with value. How can you help someone first? Typically, that's where true, genuine PR comes out. For example, you could help the newspaper by putting together an exciting story for them. You could help out an event manager by speaking on a topic that has relevance to their conference. You could give that company a shoutout on social media. Give first.

11. Develop Genuine Relationships – Go make friends. Don't be a fake friend looking to get something out of every interaction. PR is all about relationships, so focus on building strong connections with the press, influencers, and other relevant stakeholders. If you don't know how to do this, I'd recommend one of my favorite books, *How To Win Friends And Influence People* by Dale Carnegie.

12. Keep Track of PR Efforts – Take notes on PR efforts so that you can quickly refer back to them in the future if needed. What gets tracked, gets accomplished. You can

always go back and perfect your strategies after taking a look at the past data.

13. Stay Responsive – Respond promptly to queries from the press or potential clients, as this will help you build trust and credibility with them. Be *easy* to get ahold of. Answer your phone, call them back, and show interest in them as a human being. It does not always have to be strict business. Show your personality.

14. Measure PR Success – Track PR metrics such as media mentions and social shares to measure the success of your PR efforts. Similar to #12, you need to track your efforts, but also track your successes with it. Which story did the best? Which strategy are you getting some momentum with? Who has been doing a lot of the PR legwork for you?

15. Offering Incentives – Consider offering giveaways, bonuses, and other creative incentives to get people to see you differently. Everyone loves a business that has some fun, does fun things with their team, and also engages with their followers. Think outside of the box.

16. Create Engaging Content – Focus on creating engaging content that will resonate with your target audience. How can you get them involved with what you're doing? How can you capture someone's attention with the content you put out? (Hint: it doesn't always have to be about you)

17. Utilize PR Tools – Explore PR tools such as press release distribution services, media monitoring software, or PR analytics tools to make PR efforts more efficient and effective. This would be that "next step" for you as you start figuring out how it all works together. There are incredible tools out there to streamline this process and help you see everything in one place. Plus, everyone loves dashboards!

18. Track Your Competitors – Monitor what other construction companies are doing so that you can stay ahead of PR trends and create campaigns that set you apart from the competition. You may have to look outside of your area and scope it out on a national level. See what others are doing that you really resonate with. Consider even reaching out to them to talk more about what they're doing and how they like it.

19. Monitor PR Reputation – Keeping an eye on your PR reputation is essential for quickly addressing any potential issues or concerns that arise. Isn't all publicity good publicity? Not in my book. We need to make sure you are staying on top of any bad press so that you can address it if needed.

20. Plan for PR Crises – Develop a plan in advance to handle PR crises when they occur, as this will help you stay ahead of PR problems and protect your company's reputation. The odds you will need to use this are slim, but it's better to be prepared.

Don't feel like you need to do all 20 today. Public Relations is challenging and requires a commitment to a long-term strategy. You may want to work with some PR experts to get clarity on how you can best strategize for the size of your company. The most important tip I have for your PR strategy is to just be a good person and treat others well. That will take you places.

ELEVEN

PAY-PER-CLICK MARKETING (GOOGLE ADS AND BING SEARCH) - HOW TO MAXIMIZE THE PROFITABILITY OF YOUR PAY-PER-CLICK MARKETING EFFORTS

In this chapter, we're going to talk about Pay-Per-Click Marketing to help you understand how it works, why it should be integrated into your overall strategy, and how you can run an effective program that can drive profitable business to your construction company.

Why PPC Should Be Part of Your Overall Digital Marketing Strategy

- Start showing up quickly
- Show up as often as possible where potential clients are looking
- Show up for non-geo-modified terms that are related to your service offering.
- Put out more touch points for people looking for a new employer, potential partner, or a bigger source client that can give you recurring business (engineering firm, architecture, home builders, city, government, etc.)

First, PPC gets things happening quickly, unlike an SEO program, setting up your website, building links, and having the right on-page optimization. SEO takes time to materialize. What you do today and tomorrow, will start to pay dividends in four to six months. With PPC advertising, you set up your campaign and will start to see your ads serve in just a few days. It can drive good traffic, especially during the times when you need to make sure you're visible.

For a non-construction example, it would be a good strategy for flower shops to use PPC a week or so before Valentine's Day when couples are looking for a perfect gift for their Valentine. This is a great time to advertise your store because people are looking and are more likely to convert to sales.

You want to show up as often as possible when someone's looking for your services. Having a PPC ad that shows up somewhere in the top, on the map, and in the organic section is important.

This gives you the opportunity to show up in multiple places and significantly improves the chances of getting your ad clicked on. A PPC campaign gives you that additional placeholder on the search engines on page one. It also gives you the opportunity to show up for words that you're not going to show up for in your organic SEO efforts. This is what I like to call non-geo-modified keywords.

SEO and our whole organic strategy give us the ability to show up in search engines when someone types in your city service. For example, your city landscaping company, your city septic contractor, your city hydroseeding, etc. All of those include some kind of geo-modifier (your city). Your customers are going to input their city or sub-city for your site to rank.

With a PPC campaign, you can show up for the non-geo-modified terms (Example: home building, roofing, new home construction, foundation digging, lawn installs, etc.), and put in the settings that you only want to show up for people within a 25-mile radius of your office.

If you're in Miami and somebody searches within that area for "excavation contractor" or "basement digging" you can set it so that it only shows your ad for those searching within that area. Google can manage that through IP addresses by isolating where the search took place.

Google can also isolate who ran that search and where they ran that search from, then place the ads based on the viewers that are in that area.

When using PPC marketing, you only pay on a per-click basis, but you're able to show up for those keywords in those major markets. Another reason to consider running a PPC campaign is that you can run mobile PPC campaigns.

With mobile PPC campaigns, when somebody is searching for your services from a mobile device, it's typically because they need immediate service. They're not as apt to browse multiple pages or listings. Now, if somebody runs a search on their mobile device, and you have a PPC campaign set up, that search will be PPC enabled. A good example of these could be 24/7 emergency water line repair, a septic system clogged or backed up, or basement flooding. These are great call ads to set up because people want to call the first contractor they see when they're panicking and in an emergency situation.

Potential customers can simply clock on your ad and automatically be calling your company, rather than browsing your website and researching.

On a PPC campaign through mobile, you're actually paying per call as opposed to paying per lead. It's very powerful, and these are the reasons you want to have PPC as part of your overall digital marketing plan.

The Pay-Per-Click Networks

So, what are the pay-per-click networks? There are two major networks that manage PPC advertising across almost all major search engines. There are Google Ads, which is Google's PPC program, and then there is Bing, which is through Microsoft Search.

These both have their own network behind them, so when you pay for an ad or PPC campaign on Google's search network, you're gaining access to many other platforms.

Most searches happen on Google so we always recommend starting there. You can go into Bing and other search engines, but google is the dominating search engine by far. Don't overthink it, get started on Google.

Understanding the Google Ads Auction Process

Let's review how Google Ads work.

In the simplest sense, you're paying on a per-click basis and you can choose your keywords; For example, construction company, your city construction company, or your city emergency septic contractor. As you pick those words, you bid, and you pay on a per-click basis.

So, let's just say you're bidding on the keywords "Dallas Landscaping Company" and there are a lot of other landscaping companies in that city that want to rank for that keyword. If you say that you'll pay $2.00/click and your competitor says that they'll pay $5.00/click, they're going to be at the top. Assuming nobody else has placed a higher bid, $2.00 is going to be ranked second and anything less than that will follow.

However, I will now explain why that isn't 100% of the reality. The fact is that you pay on a per-click basis and you are bidding against the competitors to determine how you're going to rank on your keyword.

It's an auction, just like eBay. People are bidding and whoever can offer the most money is going to have the strongest position. With that foundational understanding, we can now explain why most PPC campaigns fail.

What tends to happen is a lot of PPC campaigns are built on the notion that the highest bid wins. So advertisers pick their keywords, throw up the highest bid per click, and hope that everything turns out the way they want it.

Why Most Pay-Per-Click Campaigns Fail

- Setup only ONE ad group for all services
- Don't use specific text ads and landing pages for groups of keywords
- No strong call to action on the landing page

You might be thinking, you just told me that PPC is a great way to get noticed, and now you're saying that most campaigns fail! I'm going to explain what people do wrong and then show you what to do right so that your campaign is successful.

Typically, businesses set up only one ad group for all services, whether it's landscaping, hydroseeding, lawn installs, retaining wall builds, or pool installs, instead of different ad groups for each type of service.

There are also no specific text ads and no landing pages for those ad groups and groups of keywords.

What you wind up with is the same landing page and the same text ad, whether your client typed in "landscaping, hydroseeding, lawn installs, retaining walls, pool contractor, etc." in the search engine.

Whatever was typed into the search engine was likely very specific, and should match up to a very specific page, but that doesn't happen. It all goes to the home page. With this strategy, not only is your campaign going to convert poorly, but your cost per click is going to be higher. I will explain why later in this chapter.

The other reason why most PPC campaigns fail is that there isn't a strong call-to-action on the landing page. So, you were just charged $5.00 or $9.00 to get a potential client to your website and the page isn't even compelling because it does not have a strong call-to-action. It doesn't tell the consumer what to do next.

If you factor in these common reasons that PPC campaigns tend to fail, you can better prepare yourself and set yourself up for success in the way that you execute your PPC marketing.

Understanding the Google Ads Auction Process

Let's talk about how the Google Ads Auction process works. It's not as simple as the highest bidder winning. It's more complicated than that.

The reality is Google needs to feature the most relevant results because its endgame is to get people to keep using their search engine over the competition. This is how they can keep their traffic up.

Google can keep its usage up and maintain that 80 percent market share but can also run Google Ads and make billions of dollars per year. Ultimately it all comes down to relevancy.

The second they sacrifice relevancy for dollars is the second they start to become less of a player in their market. So, Google had to figure out a way to make their PPC program grow around relevancy. And so that's why they established the quality score. They need to make sure that the person or company who has more relevancy gets a higher quality score and as result, can have a lower cost per click.

The way I like to explain it is if I go to Google and type in "BMW," obviously I am looking for a BMW dealer or for information about BMW.

Mercedes could say, "That's our demographic also. If someone types in BMW, they're looking for a high-end vehicle. They are probably in the market to buy. Why don't I bid on the word BMW?" Of course, they can. However, the person that searched for BMW isn't looking for Mercedes. So, Mercedes could say, "I'll pay $25.00 for everybody that clicks on me when they search 'BMW'."

But BMW might say, "That's my brand and I am going to compete for it, but I am not going to spend $25.00 for every click on my own brand. I'll pay a dollar for every click." Based on the quality score, Google may decide to serve BMW because it's in the best interest of the person researching the brand, the consumer. It's also in the best interest of overall relevancy. That's how the quality score works. Quality score is really driven by three core components:

- Click Through Rate
- Relevance
- Quality of Landing page

As somebody conducts a search and your website shows up on the page in the PPC section, Google is tracking what percentage of those people saw your ad and wound up clicking through.

That's one of the primary metrics that they analyze. So, if your ad is relevant, if it speaks to the person's needs, and if it's compelling enough to them that they click through, Google just made more per click. This will help Google give you a higher quality score because you have a better click-through rate.

Also, relevancy is a major factor. How relevant is your text ad to the keyword that was typed? For example, someone types in "hydroseeding" and your text ad reads: "We're the best landscaping contractor in the Dallas area," versus "We're the best landscaping contractor in the Dallas area and we offer high-quality hydroseeding services in the Dallas area." Which do you think is more relevant to the client? Google wants its search results to be as applicable as possible. They're looking at your click-through rate, the relevancy of your text ad to your keywords, and the quality of your landing page.

If your landing page (the page that you drive people to) doesn't match with what the person just clicked based on your text ad, or if that landing page doesn't have a strong call-to-action and the person quickly returns to the search engine, that signals to Google that you were not very relevant.

This will result in a quality score reduction.

By having a higher quality score, you can bid lower and still achieve the top position. This is where you can win in the PPC marketing game because a better-quality score results in a lower cost-per-click for those who hold the top positions.

Most PPC campaigns fail, it's because they only set up one ad group, they have a weak call-to-action, or they high have a high click-through rate. All of these issues result in a lower quality score and result in paying more per click. PPC marketing is very competitive. If you're paying more per click, you're not going to be able to spend that much because you won't be getting enough calls to generate a return on investment.

The visual representation of this would be like setting up one Google Ads campaign for each one of these services (landscaping, hydroseeding, lawn installs, retaining walls, pool contractor, etc.) and landing people on your home page. That is a recipe for disaster.

It's extremely powerful to connect with these people that are searching from mobile devices. Set up a mobile-specific campaign and choose "Mobile Devices Only." Then you can pick your geolocation, which is your 30-mile range or 20-mile radius, and turn on the click-to-call function.

These steps help you set up a PPC campaign that has you in the top positions if you bid correctly and a stronger conversion with a click-to-call.

To recap, it is important to do the following when launching a PPC campaign:

- Set up your ad groups correctly
- Make sure that you pick keywords that group them together

- Write text ads that speak directly to that group of keywords
- Ensure your landing page (where you are sending those specific searches) speaks to the text ads and the group of keywords
- Have a strong call-to-action that prompts your consumer into calling you as opposed to pressing the "Back" button and looking at four or five other competitors

As the relevancy of your ad groups campaign and your keywords improve, your cost-per-click will decline and your conversion will improve.

You can spend less and still get better positioning and more traffic to your website. This is how you maximize the profitability of your PPC marketing campaigns and succeed where others fail.

TWELVE

Track, Measure AND Quantify - How to track your digital marketing plan to ensure that your investment is generating a strong return on investment

When it comes to online marketing, construction companies need to ensure that their investment is generating a strong return on investment. The first step towards this goal is tracking and measuring your progress. This can help you identify areas for improvement, understand the effectiveness of your campaigns, and evaluate how much value you are getting from your budget. Here are some tips for tracking and measuring your online marketing plan for construction companies:

Set Clear Goals

Before you begin any digital marketing, it's important to set clear goals so that you have something to measure against as you move forward. This could be anything from increasing website traffic or building brand awareness to creating leads or driving employment applications - just make sure your goals are specific and measurable. Maybe you are looking to rank in the number one spot on Google for X amount of keywords. Whatever your goals are, write them down and keep them clear.

Track Performance Metrics

Once your goals are in place, regularly track performance metrics such as website visits, page views, time spent on each page, and conversion rates. Doing this will provide valuable insight into the success of each campaign so you can focus on what works best. Additionally consider setting up A/B tests with different variables so that you can see which versions perform better before launching fully fleshed-out campaigns.

Monitor Social Media Engagement

As we talked about earlier, social media provides a great platform for interacting directly with potential clients, but it's not enough to simply post content. You can take it a step further and begin monitoring engagement closely in order to maximize your reach. Analyze likes, comments, and shares regularly in order to determine which types of content resonate most with your followers so that you can focus on creating more of these posts going forward. You may notice that short-form videos of your dozers, excavators, and skids out in the field will perform better than a graphic you put together. Social media algorithms will show your content to more people if it is what the people actually want to see.

Quantify Results

Measuring KPIs such as website visits from social sources or ROI from campaigns will give a better indication of the outcomes generated by each strategy implemented. Additionally, consider implementing tools such as Google Analytics (mentioned below) or other tracking scripts that allow you to quantify results accurately and capture detailed data about the user behavior when people interact with your website or social media channels.

When done correctly, tracking and measuring your digital marketing plan provides invaluable insight into what's working (and what isn't) so that you can adjust according accordingly in order to maximize the return on your investment over time.

Analytics Tracking

There are a lot of different tracking mechanisms that you can put in place. I'm going to recommend three core tracking mechanisms:

- Google Analytics
- Keyword Tracking
- Call Tracking

The first is Google Analytics. Google Analytics is a great website data analysis tool and it's completely free. Google Analytics will show you specifically:

- How many visitors got to your website on a daily, weekly, monthly, and annual basis
- What keywords they typed in to get there
- What pages on your website they visited
- How long they stayed

The main thing you want to see from Google Analytics is where you started and where you are now.

You want to ask yourself: When I started this whole digital marketing process, how many visitors were coming to my website? Whether it was 5, 20, 100, or 500, it is important to know your baseline. Then you can compare to future data on an ongoing basis.

Ultimately, what you are looking for is whether or not the number of visitors to your website is increasing. Is the variety of keywords that they're finding you with increasing? Are you moving in a positive direction?

How to Set Up a Google Analytics Tracking System For Website Visits & Page Views

Google Analytics is one of the most popular tracking tools available - and setting it up can help provide valuable insights into how visitors are engaging with your website. To properly set up Google Analytics, construction companies need to first create an account and then implement analytics code snippets into the HTML of their site. Here are some tips on how to do this:

Create An Account

The first step is creating an account with Google Analytics. Go to google.com/analytics and sign in with your existing Google credentials or create a new account if necessary. Once signed in, click "Admin" on the left-hand menu, select "Create Account" from the dropdown, fill out all relevant information, and click save at the bottom of the page once completed.

Implement Code Snippets

Once you have created an account, it's time to install code snippets on your website so that data can be accurately tracked and analyzed over time. To do this, click "Admin" again from the left-hand menu and select "Tracking Info" from the dropdown; then click "Tracking Code" under "Website Tracking" which will display a block of code that needs to be added in either your header or footer template (depending on your CMS). Insert this code into all pages of your site that you would like to track; make sure you test out different versions before going live as this ensures accuracy when measuring metrics such as pageviews or session duration etc..

Link Your Ad Accounts

If there are any online campaigns being run for your construction business, consider linking them to Google Analytics for more detailed reporting around performance metrics such as cost per acquisition (CPA) or return on investment (ROI). To do this, head back over to the Admin panel where you'll find options under Advertising Reporting; simply link all relevant accounts here by following each platform's instructions before completing the setup.

Setting up a Google Analytics tracking system takes just a few steps but makes a huge difference - having access to accurate data can help construction businesses better measure their progress against specific goals and ensure they are getting maximum value from their online marketing investment!

Keyword Tracking

The other tracking mechanism that I recommend is keyword tracking. At the beginning of this process, we talked about keyword research to determine what keywords people are typing in when they need your services.

We came up with a list and all those keywords were combined with your cities and sub-cities.

There are tools that will tell you how you're ranking on Google, Yahoo, and Bing for those various keywords. A few options include:

- Bright Local
- SEMRush
- Raven Tools
- WebCEO

The keyword tracking tool I recommend is called BrightLocal (www.brightlocal.com). There is a cost associated with this service, but it is a great resource for tracking your search engine optimization progress.

To use the program, you put your keywords into the BrightLocal Keyword Tracker and then set up a weekly and monthly report that shows where you rank on Google, Yahoo, and Bing for your most important keywords.

With a report like this, you can easily see how your website is trending in the search engines. You'll see yourself move up in the results if you've built out the website correctly with the right on-page factors (title tags, H1 tags, meta descriptions, etc.), if you're building links, developing citations, and have a proactive review acquisition system in place.

If you see yourself stagnating, you can go back to that keyword, figure out which page is optimized for it, look at your links and link profile, and leverage the strategies covered in this bookto push that keyword to the next level.

Call Tracking

The third really important tracking mechanism that I recommend is call tracking. Having better rankings and more visits to your website is great and all, but in most businesses, nothing happens until a call is made.

Calls are crucial to your business. You want to have some type of tracking mechanism in place to know how many calls are coming in on a monthly basis and what's happening within those conversations.

Are calls turning into sales, applications for employment, or potential brand deals? That's where the rubber meets the road. That's why we're doing all of this.

There are several call-tracking tools that you can use. Here are a few:

- CallFire
- DialogTech
- CallSource
- Century Interactive

One of the tools I've seen used prevalently is called CallFire (www.CallFire.com). Most of these call-tracking services will let you choose a phone number based on your area code. So, you type in the number you want to get. It's a nominal fee on a monthly basis ($2 - $5 per month), and you get a tracking number.

Then you can take that tracking phone number and you can put it on the graphics on your website so that you can track the number of calls and even listen to recordings of the conversation.

That number will be set to ring in your office. It's just a forwarding number. If somebody dials it, it still rings to your office like always, but it is a tracking number.

You can report the number of calls using the Internet and play back recordings of those conversations. It's extremely powerful to know the number of calls you were getting when you started versus the number after you incorporated your new marketing strategy.

You can also listen to those conversations and ascertain how many of those calls turned into booked services while knowing what the revenue associated with that service is. That is how you get a true gauge of the return on investment associated with your online marketing strategy.

There are a lot of different things you can do, but having analytics, keyword tracking, and call tracking gives you the most important key performance indicators to gauge your progress.

THIRTEEN

Wrapping up

Throughout this book, we have covered a TON of information. I know I mentioned it in the beginning, but you need to make sure that you are delegating. Do not try and do everything yourself. Like I always say, you can make a lot more money running a construction company and not fiddling around with digital marketing. This book is to help grow your foundational knowledge of what's involved in a digital marketing strategy. I highly recommend not taking all of this on yourself as the quality of execution will be poor *and* you will burn yourself out. There are people you can hire, contractors you can bring on, marketing agencies dedicated to construction companies (phasermarketing.com), and tons of resources to assist you so that you don't have to master it all yourself.

We've mapped out your digital marketing plan and taken you step-by-step through how to claim and optimize your Google map listing, how to optimize your website for the most commonly searched keywords in your area, and how to leverage social media to build a more sustainable brand to attract new employees, clients, and partnerships.

We then covered paid online marketing strategies like pay-per-click campaigns. With all of these channels set up and rolling, you should be well on your way to dominating the search engines for the keywords in your area.

Want to take your construction company to the next level?

If you've gotten to this point, THANK YOU. This book includes a lot of technical terminology and acronyms that you might have never heard of. It is 100% okay to not understand it all or feel overwhelmed with all that is possible. I always tell people that I want to be a resource first and a marketing agency second. Writing "The Digital Dirt World" has given me the chance to continue doing my best to be a resource for you and the construction industry as a whole. I would love to hear from you and get you connected with our other resources and events including the Dirt Bags Podcast, Dirt Bags University, Dirt Work Marketing, Crew Collaborative, The Phaser Fundraiser, Phaser Marketing Trades Scholarship, The Polar Plunge, Turf Wars Racing, and many others!

Please feel free to text or call me directly at (218)234-7345 if you'd be interested in working with Phaser Marketing. Our team at Phaser will take a look into your website and marketing efforts, and do a full SEO audit to see how we can help. We *only* do digital marketing for construction companies and we aren't going to be slowing down anytime soon. If you want to take that next step and increase your online visibility, give me a call or jump on our website to learn more and stay up to date with everything we are doing at Phaser Marketing. God Bless!

Phaser Marketing Website: phasermarketing.com

Podcast: dirtbagspodcast.com

Phone Number: (218) 234-7345

Find Luke Eggebraaten and Phaser Marketing on all social channels: LinkedIn, TikTok, Facebook, and Instagram.

Let's Go!